White American Pelicans.
Pelecanus erythrorhynchos
Photographed at the
Riverlands Audubon Conservation Area in
St. Charles, Missouri, May 5, 2013

Dedication:

To Martin, to whom I am eternally grateful.
Since "eternally grateful" only lasts 30 seconds,
I have had to calculate how many times I have had to
renew the 30 seconds. Over 20 years, it amounts to
twenty million, seven hundred and twenty six thousand.
(Well, it's a lot anyway).
Thank you Martin,
I could never have gotten good pictures
without your enthusiasm.

Marian Brickner

Whimsical Animal Photographer., has pictures
published in:
Frans de Waal's The Bonobo and the Atheist",
"I'm Lucy: A Day in the Life of a Young Bonobo" ,
by Mathea Levine, afterword by
Jane Goodall, Produced by Ursula Goodenough
"Growing Up Bonobo" by Tracy Fenn
The Empathy Way Series, written by Anne Paris:
"Insides Out", "I'm Different, You're Different," "You Scared Me",
and a Teacher's Manual.
Richard Milner's "Darwin A to Z"
Produced by Marian:
"Animals Don't Wear Lipstick", "What's a Family Anyway",
"Seasoned Dogs," "Paws on a Line, Claws and Hoofs Too",
"A Tale of Dales", " Mutts and Rascals", "With Bright Shiny Faces",
"Birds of a Feather", "Trumpeter Swan Family". and more.

www.marianbricknerphotography.com

Someone in here has a fish.

Possible sharing probabilities?

It's in here somewhere.

She has the fish.

FISH

An Asian Carp no less!

Fish

Fish

Fish

Fish is in here!

Fish

Where's the fish?

Fish in there.

Fish in here!

Somehow, she managed to scoot around to the
back of the group preparing to swallow her fish.

Fish is being swallowed.

Pretty well all gone!

The American White Pelican is about four feet tall and has a wingspan of about NINE feet. It is entirely white except for its black-edged wings that are visible when the American White Pelican is in flight. The pelican doesn't dive into the water for its food. It floats on the water and scoops up fish and water into its pouch. (The real name for the pouch is GULAR. The GULAR is DISTENSIBLE.) As you can see in these pictures it can get very big to hold a big fish.
The images in this book are a series of pictures taken while a particular pelican has caught a fish and her/his "friends" seem to be wanting to get it for themselves.

www.ingramcontent.com/pod-product-compliance
Lightning Source LLC
Chambersburg PA
CBHW040203240726
48664CB00002B/820